BERLIN

Ingo and Claudia Latotzki

Contents

Preface

1. The new Berlin: the Sony Center (designed by Helmut Jahn) on Potsdam Square (Potsdamer Platz)

2. This tower, on Potsdam Square (Potsdamer Platz), belongs to the Deutsche Bahn (the German national railway company)

The Germans have a saying: 'No matter the distance, Berlin is always worth the journey'. This is even truer today. Since the Fall of the Berlin Wall, this city on the river Spree with its 3.5 million inhabitants has been enjoying unparalleled development. One example of the German capital's transformation is the semi-futuristic architecture of the Potsdamer Platz, which is currently Europe's biggest building site.

Two recent dates are assured a place in the history of Berlin: 3 October 1990 when 100,000 people gathered in front of the Reichstag to celebrate the reunification of Germany and 9 November 1989, the day on which the border opened for the first time. The change in politics has certainly enriched the cultural life of the city: there are 170 museums, more than 200 theatres and cinemas, three national opera houses, 160 art galleries, 880 choirs and eight major orchestras.

This is a city that never sleeps: there are 2,000 licensed pubs plus countless bars, restaurants and bistros. Yet should you wish to escape the noise, you only have to go a few stops on the underground to find yourself in green surroundings: nearly a third of Berlin's surface consists in parks, forests and water. Another advantage of the underground system is that it links the world famous sites in the city centre with those in the outlying districts: for example the Brandenburg Gate, the Kurfürstendamm,

the Berliner Dom, and the Schloss Charlottenburg. 'No matter the distance, Berlin is always worth the journey.' Another saying is 'I always keep a suitcase in Berlin'. Is there any better way to express one's affection for a city?

3. Futuristic architecture on Potsdam Square: the tower of the DB (the German national railway company)

4. The capital is in constant construction: cranes in the government quarter

Berlin is a relatively young metropolis

An excursion into history

5. The Television Tower (Funkturm), in the Mitte quarter (Center), which is an ancient East-German symbol

6. Equestrian statue of Friedrich der Große (Frederic the Great) on the sumptuous boulevard called "Unter den Linden"

Berlin is still a relatively young metropolis. The first recorded reference to the village of Cölln is in 1237. After the union with Berlin (1307), situated on the opposite bank of the river Spree, the town grew rapidly. Under the Elector of Brandenburg the city became a trading centre then the capital of Prussia, and later of a united Germany. Following the Second World War and the Berlin Agreement, Berlin became the focus of the "Cold War". Two years after the Fall of the Berlin Wall in 1989, the city on the Spree again became the capital of Germany.

Although human remains have been found in Berlin dating from 8000 BC, the first permanent settlement was in the thirteenth century. On the south bank of the river Spree was the fishing village Cölln, and on the north was Berlin. To mark their union, both villages joined to build the Town Hall on the Lange Brücke, the long bridge that spanned the river. They were equally united in their resistance against the Hohenzollerns. However, the independence of both towns ended in 1447–48 when the Hohenzollerns successfully defeated a popular uprising. The citizens had protested against the building of a Hohenzollern palace and the loss of their civil liberties, and it all ended in bloodshed.

Now the expansion of the city as a princely domain could begin. Berlin became a fortress and the most important trading port between Breslau and Hamburg, both during the reign of the Elector Friedrich Wilhelm (1640–1688).

7. In memory of the Jewish victims of the Holocaust on Grosse Hamburger Strasse road
8. A Soviet Memorial for the 300 000 soldiers who died during the Second World War in the battle over Berlin

In 1685 the Elector granted religious freedom and the right to settle to the persecuted Huguenots – the Potsdam Edict. This resulted in a crucial period of growth, but it was only under Friedrich II (1740–1786) that Berlin became a European city.

The city on the Spree became a centre of the Enlightenment after Frederick the Great's modernisation of law and administration, the establishment of factories, and the abolition of torture. He also fought for religious tolerance. Due to his successful military campaigns, Prussia grew by almost two thirds. When 'Old Fritz' as he was affectionately known, died, Berlin had 150,000 inhabitants and was, after London and Paris, the third largest city of Europe.

Under Friedrich Wilhelm III (1797–1840) Berlin became the largest industrial city in Europe, and after victories against Denmark and Austria, Prussia was the leading power in Germany. In 1871 the German princes offered Wilhelm I the Imperial crown and Berlin became the capital of the new German Empire. Otto von Bismarck was the Chancellor and it was he who was the driving force behind the 'foundation years' with the building of factories and grand houses. At the same time, however, the poverty of the working classes, who had to live in dark, rented barracks, rapidly increased. A new industrial era had begun in Berlin. At the same time the population exploded: in 1877 Berlin had one million inhabitants, and by 1905 the number had doubled. This period also saw a great increase in technical achievements: in 1876 a new sewage system was built; 1897 saw the introduction of electric street lighting; the first telephones were used in 1881 and a year later the first tram made its maiden journey.

A Megalomaniac Vision

The First World War ended in a German defeat that paved the way for the Weimar Republic. This could also be called the Berlin Republic since the city witnessed both the birth and the death of the German democracy. In the Twenties Berlin was the artistic capital of Europe. However, this was only for a short time. Social tensions increased with the rise of inflation and the world economic crisis, while the political climate of radicalism and party infighting prepared the ground for the National Socialists to take power. Adolf Hitler moved swiftly to abolish the old institutions, replacing them with the "Ermächtigungsgesetz" (Enabling Legislation) on 23 March 1933. This was the beginning of the Third Reich. Megalomaniacs now made plans for Berlin to have grandiose buildings suitable for a world capital to be called Germania. To implement this terrible vision six million Jews were murdered. The end of the Second World War and the Nazi Regime left Berlin a city in ruins with 1.5 million of its 4.3 million inhabitants dead or missing. Germany was divided up among the four victorious powers: the USA, England, France and the Soviet Union, and Berlin was ruled by a council of the Allies. It was not long before the political climate changed again. The Allied Forces that had joined together against the Nazi terror were now divided: in 1948 the Soviet Union left the Allied Council and a blockade of West Berlin began on 24 June.

9. The subway station Französische Strasse on Friedrichstrasse road, surrounded by the city's new consumer temples
10. The new Sony Center with its imposing architecture designed by Helmut Jahn
11. The Brandenburg Gate by night

Following pages:
12. The golden dome of the Neue Synagoge on the Oranienburger Strasse

13. The walls of the Hackesche Höfe (renovated courtyards):
they were built at the beginning of the 20th century
by Kurt Berndt and August Endell, two architects who
participated in the German Jugendstil (the 1900 style)
14. A moment of relaxation near the Hackesche Höfe
15. A new SMS? A young girl on the Ku'damm boulevard

The Cold War era had begun. For almost a year the city had to be supplied by air, and in 1949 the separation was finalised with the founding of two states on German soil – one in the East and the other in the West. When Berlin became a divided city, it was originally without walls or barbed wire to secure the border. A people's revolt in East Berlin on 17 June 1953 was met by Soviet tanks and was cruelly suppressed. In 1961 the SED (United Socialist Party) walled up its state after hundreds of thousands had fled from the GDR (German Democratic Republic). Many thought that this would be the end of Berlin; but they were wrong. The Federal Republic was supporting the western part of Berlin with billions of deutschmarks in subsidies. Soon the Wall became a part of everyday life and hardly anyone believed that it would ever go away. The SED party leader and head of state, Erich Honecker, declared that it would stand more than 100 years. The man was wrong. After a peaceful revolution in the former GDR, the Wall was breached on 9 November 1989. Socialism had failed. Berlin however, remained a legally divided city. It was not until 4 March 1991 that Germany and Berlin regained their full sovereignty with the introduction of the 'Two-plus-four Contract'.

Disputed Agreement

On 20 June 1990, after stormy debates and by a margin of only eight votes, the Bundestag agreed that Berlin should again become the seat of government and of parliament in Germany. Investors and speculators immediately saw the economic possibilities in this decision and vast building projects were launched. Some have by now become remarkable sites. The area around Potsdamer Platz, which on the GDR side was wasteland, became the largest building site in Europe financed by global companies. For over a year cranes dominated the landscape. The city had never experienced such a massive project and the giant site has been transformed into a unique district. The first building to be opened was the Daimler-Crysler complex by Renzo Piano and Christoph Kohlbecker at the southern end of the site. North is the Sony Center, designed by Helmut Jahn with a futuristic roof, rather like a circus tent, spanning the inner court. The Sony Center could be regarded as a minor landmark. Built in a semi circle, it is especially splendid at night when the glass façades radiate a green light. A part of the former Grand Hotel Esplanade has been integrated in the Sony Center. The cost of the whole project amounts to 25 million euros.

Not only are there architectural masterpieces here for the visitor to admire, but there is much else in the way of entertainment: cinemas, musical theatres, arcades, casinos, elegant boutiques, bistros and restaurants can all be found in the Potsdamer Platz. Facing the Sony Tower is another architectural jewel, an office building designed by Kohloff and Timmermann. The clinker brickwork reminds us of trading houses in the North German ports. The star architects of the Potsdamer Platz have made many efforts to combine their visionary building strategy with the elements of living, shopping and recreation. How well they have succeeded! At Leipzig Platz and Paris Platz more building work is taking place. The new Berlin has devoured incredible sums of money. From 1994 to the beginning of the new millennium, 140 billion euros were invested in buildings, while another 100 billion were used in the modernisation and restoration of the infrastructure.

16. When the clock strikes: the world clock on Alexander Place (Alexanderplatz), which is 10 metres high
17. The city's symbol: a Berliner bear on the Kurfürstendamm boulevard

North of the centre of Berlin, in the Scheunenviertel, intensive building work is also underway to beautify this area which translates as 'the Barn Quarter'. In 1672 the Great Elector ordered that all the barns should be put outside the city walls to minimize the risk of fire. Thereafter the area became home to many immigrant communities, including many Jewish families. In Oranienburg Strasse the Neue Synagogue with its gilded dome is to be found. This splendid building was opened in the presence of Chancellor Otto von Bismark in 1866. After German Unification the whole quarter experienced a revival. Bars, cafes, pubs and restaurants sprung up and they say that nowhere in the eastern part of Berlin will you find a more exciting nightlife. Once you are there, it is worthwhile exploring the restored Hackesche Höfe. Erected at the beginning of the twentieth century to the designs of two leading exponents of the Jugendstil style, Kurt Berndt and August Endell, the building consists of a series of courtyards with elegant façades. The first courtyard is particularly attractive with glazed tiles arranged in colourful geometric patterns covering all the walls.

Among the many cultural masterpieces that were out of bounds to visitors before 1989, some are to be found in the Nicolaiviertel, close to Alexander Platz. Apart from the 365m-tall television tower (a former symbol of the GDR), you will find some of the oldest houses in the city which survived the Second World War, lining the banks of the river Spree. The efforts of GDR's leaders to restore these houses in the style of a medieval town were a doubtful success. However, in the countless narrow lanes, pub and restaurant owners are doing their best to entice visitors.

There is history at almost every corner

Due to recent historical events, the Berlin Dom, one of the most grandiose buildings in East Berlin, has become again a normal stop with the city tours. This protestant cathedral was the court church and mausoleum of the Hohenzollerns, but the design of the present building dates from the 1890s. The earlier designs were by the famous architects, Karl Friedrich Schinkel and Johann Boumann. In contrast to today's building with its 85m-high copper plated dome, the first design by Boumann from the 1740s looks rather modest. In 1816–1821, Schinkel altered the Cathedral in the classical style.

The present building is by Julius Raschdorff, dating from 1894–1905. During the War the Berlin Dom suffered tremendous damage and stands today in a simpler form without the mausoleum.

The sarcophagus of the first King of Prussia, Friedrich I and his wife, designed by Andreas Schlüter, are resting in the Berlin Dom. Friederich was ambitious and an art lover. Under his reign, in the beginning of the eighteenth century, the Zeughaus, the Academy of Arts, and later Schloss Charlottenburg were built.

Although Berlin is a relatively young city in comparison to others, there is history to be found around every corner of the Spree Metropolis. It is a joining of old and new. How does the saying go? Nobody can understand the present, without knowing about the past.

18. The television tower stretches out behind the Berlin Cathedral
19. Berliner bears on the Unter den Linden boulevard

Following pages:
20. A pleasure for the eyes: the Berlin Cathedral was built in its present state by Julius Raschdorff between 1894 and 1905

An overview of the city: see the sights in 45 minutes

A Journey on Bus 100

'Berlin is worth the journey.' The city on the river Spree has 3.5 million inhabitants, which makes it by far the largest city in Germany (almost two million live in the former West Berlin.) Should you wish to cross Berlin, you will travel 40km, which would take you hours; and that brings us to our subject – the Bus 100. This is the ideal way to explore the German capital. Every few minutes there is a Bus 100 leaving a bus stop, and even in the evenings it keeps on running. The tour links Bezirk Mitte with Charlottenburg, which is the typical East-West axis.

So what is so special about Line 100? The double-decker bus allows you to view a great number of sights in one go and is a reasonable alternative to the conventional city tours. During the 45-minute journey the Bus 100 will pass the Brandenburg Gate, the Reichstag, the splendid Unter den Linden lined with historic buildings, like the Berliner Dom, and the Zeughaus, the Funkturm (television tower), Alexander Platz, Siegessäule (Victory Column), Schloss Bellevue, and the Kurfürstendamm. If you are quick and manage to secure a place on the upper deck of the bus, you can feast your eyes on one sight after the other. Ideally you begin your journey at the starting point, or at the last stop (Zoologischer Garten/Michelangelostrasse). This will increase your chances of getting a front seat. You can either purchase a single ticket (2.12 euros), which is valid for two hours, or a day ticket (6.10 euros).

21. The Zeughaus is considered to be one of Germany's most beautiful baroque buildings. It dates back to 1706 and was originally a weapons storage site

22. The concert hall (on the left), built by Karl Friedrich Schinkel, and the French cathedral in the Gendarmenmarkt (the Policemen's Market), the old-eastern part of the city

23. Two symbols in one: the Berliner bear and the Brandenburg Gate

24. The end of the seperation: in November 1989, people danced
    on the wall near the Brandenburg Gate
25. You can see the Brandenburg Gate wherever you go. Here,
    it is found on a bus
26. Coffee-break on the Unter den Linden boulevard. In the beginning,
    the boulevard was used by horsemen to go to the Tiergarten (zoo),
    an ancient hunting-ground

27. A coffee-place at Checkpoint Charlie: here, people can read
the Neues Deutschland (the New Germany), the old East-German
newspaper
28. Drinking a beer on the Unter den Linden boulevard to beat
the summer heat
29. A well-deserved break near the Red Townhall
30. Taking a rest in the Lustgarden (the Pleasure Parc)

As the Bus 100 runs very frequently, you can jump off the bus every now and then to see one of the sights, and then continue later at your leisure. A good stopping place would be the Tiergarten, the 'green lung' of Berlin, highly popular with both visitors and residents alike. Another advantage of this bus line is that the local people are also using it. If you speak German, this might give you the chance to learn a few things about the local dialect. For instance, do you know what a 'Falscher Hase' (false hare) is? This is what Berliners call a meat-loaf. Or a 'Boulette'? Elsewhere in Germany this is called a 'Frikadelle'. 'Boulett' comes from the French, Boule, which means a ball, and in English this is a hamburger. Alternatively, you might discover on your journey where the very best curry sausages are to be found in the city. Berlin claims to have invented this combination. Apparently, Chancellor Schroeder will indulge in one a week… And by the way, there are 1,500 snack bars in Berlin. With any luck the bus driver can point you in the right direction.

135,000 students

It is not documented whether the Mayor of Berlin is also a sausage-enthusiast, but the Bus 100 does pass by City Hall. This is where the city's destiny is made – a city that also heads the 16 states that make up the Federal Republic of Germany. Berlin also is an important city for industry and science. It has 18 universities and colleges with a total of 135,000 students. Our tour takes us past the historic and highly respected Humboldt University, which is situated on the famous Unter den Linden in the eastern part of the city. Not far away is the Museuminsel (Museum island), which is home to the arts. The city takes great pride in its exceptional collections. How many cinemas the bus passes is not known, but there are more than 200 in Berlin. Another unknown fact is the number of trees on the route. It has been said that there are more than 400,000 trees in the city and only a few are in the street Unter den Linden. The traveller on the Bus 100 may also note the contrast between modern futuristic architecture and historical buildings. This is predominantly to be found in the eastern part of the city. Towards the end of the tour, near the Prenzlau Allee, you will find old buildings dating from GDR times. Not far from there is the Hackesche Viertel which combines new, imaginative architecture with old buildings.

Once again, more contrasts. At the beginning of the third millennium we still find industrial buildings in use. The night-time traveller on Bus 100 will find Unter den Linden even more appealing when the splendid historic buildings are illuminated. So, take the Bus 100 and experience Berlin. A very worthwhile journey!

31. This palace used to be the royal and imperial heirs' residence; the original building dates back to the 17th century
32. Aerial view of the city
33. The Bellevue Castle (Schloss Bellevue): this building, with its classical facade (1785–1790), is currently the president's residence

Berlin's shopping streets: unlimited choice for the customer

The perfect city for a shopping spree

34. The Radio Tower (Funkturm) on Alexander Place (Alexanderplatz) was built during the time of state council's president Walter Ulbricht's mandate; it is also called "Saint Walter" since a cross-like-figure appears in the dome when the sun shines

35. The Column of Victory was erected following Johann Heinrich Strack's drawings, in memory of the victory of the Prusso-Danish war of 1864

There are people who only have one thing in mind when they come to Berlin: shopping. The city on the Spree certainly has to offer everything that one could desire. But where to go? – Kurfürstendamm or Tauentzienstrasse? – Potsdamer Platz or Friedrichstrasse? – and this is only a selection. Those who want to face the crowds should allow a lot of time and, in line with their objectives, money.

Let us begin our shopping trip on the respectable and renowned Kurfürstendamm. When Berlin was still a divided city, the 'Ku'damm' had no competition. It was legendary. This street was not only the shopping mile, but it was a prime business address and a smart boulevard. In the New Berlin the Ku'damm faces enormous competition. The Olympic motto: 'Higher, faster, wider' has become true for the department stores on Potsdamer Platz and Friedrichstrasse. Everything has to be chic, posh and exclusive. But competition stirs up business. Therefore the long walk down the Ku'damm is still worthwhile. Whatever you want, you can be sure of finding it here; and there are special offers everywhere. You can find expensive boutiques far beyond the budget of normal visitors and medium range shops, which are far more tempting for the tourists and their credit cards; bookshops, pubs, restaurants, furniture stores, jewellery boutiques, cinemas, theatres and much, much more. In short: the Ku'damm is still an obligatory part of any shopping program.

Situated between Uhlandstrasse and Leibnitz-strasse, right in the middle of the Kurfürstendamm, you will find world famous names as Gucci, Jil Sandler and Escada. Others can also be found in the side streets, such as Fasanenstrasse or Bleibtreustrasse. Between Uhlandstrasse and Gedächniskirche well-known stores like Benetton predominate. While at the western end, beyond Adenauerplatz and towards 'the business mile', you will find estate agents, tax advisors and lawyers. Ambitious building projects prove that the street is not on the decline, as the new Kranzler-Eck, or the Ku'damm Eck, bear witness.

Those who care to take a stroll down the 'shopping mile' in the direction of Wittenberbplatz will have no problem in getting to the Tauentzienstrasse. There you will find the world-renowned store, the Kaufhaus des Westens, KaDeWe, the department store of West Berlin.

36. The Red Townhall is the seat of the Bundesland (State of Berlin) government
37. A violinist on Ku'damm boulevard

Following pages:
38. A colourful scenery: a statue in front of the Red Townhall
39. The University of Humboldt was built in 1753 by the Prince Henry of Prussia, the brother of Frederic the Great
40. Topped with whipped cream: the famous Kranzler café on Kurfürstendamm

41. Modern architecture on Ku'damm boulevard
42. Das Kaufhaus des Westens (the Great Western Store): this is the second-largest store in the world and was considered to be a symbol of capitalism in ancient East-Germany

Before the opening of the Wall, it was seen as a symbol of capitalism by the East, particularly on account of its extensive delicatessen department located on the sixth floor. Europe's largest department store opened in 1907 and was designed by the architect Emil Schaudt. Every day there are 80,000 visitors who come to enjoy this shopping experience; others come just to browse. This temple of consumption was destroyed during the war, but it reopened on 3 July 1950. The local press described the opening day as a day when 'Women fought like wild animals over the merchandise'. Opposite the KaDeWe are quite a few beggars and homeless people. This is the other side of consumerism, which has become normal for any big city like Berlin.

A breath of New York

Were it not for the many shops with attractive, and some-times bizarre window displays that compel you to stop and take another look, it would not take very long to get to the Europa-Center. In fact it is only a few minutes away from Gedächniskirche. This centre opened in 1965. According to Willy Brandt, former Mayor of Berlin, it brought a breath of New York to the Spree. Even today it is an impressive skyscraper with 22 floors and with the Mercedes logo on the roof. The centre's promoter, Karl-Heinz Pepper, commissioned the architects Helmut Hentrich and Hubert Petschnigg to design this building, the façades of which have recently been renovated. Not only does it provide a home for cinemas, an Irish Pub, various shops and offices, but it is also home to the famous cabaret 'Die Stachelschweine' – The Porcupines.

A few stops on the underground (U-Bahn) will take you to Friedrichstrasse, which has become the new, yet old, centre of Berlin, a decade after the destruction of the Wall, symbolising many of the changes that have taken place since 1989. The sophisticated Friedrich-strasse is a fashionable place for a stroll. Since the German Reunification almost 100,000 square metres of shop-ping space have been created. By way of comparison, the KaDeWe has only 60,000 square metres. The Federal Government has invested 2 billion euros in urban development schemes in the area between Checkpoint Charly and Bahnhof Friedrichstrasse.

There is a section of street between Leipziger Strasse and Unter den Linden named Aufschwung Ost or 'Upswing of the East'. Quartiers 205, 206 and 207 in the Friedrichstadt Passagen are linked by a 260 m long underground passage. These three shopping malls contain over a 100 shops. Here too, everything is on offer: fashion designers, couture designers, but also something for the ordinary purse. This area has become a focus point for tourists as it offers other attractions as well, notably the former border crossing, Checkpoint Charlie, and a museum which is well worth seeing. Nearby there is the Gendarmenmarkt where you will find the Französischer Dom and the Deutsche Dom framing the Konzerthaus. A special attraction in Quartier 207 are the Lafayette Galleries a branch of the Parisian department store, designed by the French architect, Jean Nouvel. This building is full of elegance and lightness through the use of vast amounts of glass both on the outside and on the inside of the building.

43. Dolls in the store window of the Friedrichstrasse
44. A store window in the Scheunenviertel (the Barn quarter)

Another attraction is the Lichthof, or Court of Light. This consists of two large glass cones, which together rise to 37 m in height in the Friedrichstadt Passagen, that radiate light. The neighbouring Quartier 206 consists of offices and boutiques. It bears the signature of the American architects, Pei, Cobb, Freed & Partners who have created an impressive façade with hundreds of optical patterns. The interior is luxurious and extravagant. There are expensive marble ornaments on the walls, as well as on the floors, and the spectacular hall has been designed in Art Deco style. The biggest shopping mall is Quartier 205, designed by Oswald Mathias Ungers, and is the most modest-looking building.

45. Another symbol: the church in memory of Kaiser-Wilhelm; besides it stands the new hexagonal clock-tower
46. View of the Memorial Church through the Berlin sculpture, which symbolizes the union of Germany

A metropolis of culture: 170 museums, 880 choirs and 260 art galleries

Berlin: An Art Form...

As with shopping, you are also spoilt for choice when it comes to cultural choices in Berlin. Among the 170 museums there is the world famous Pergamon Museum, and the Jewish Museum in Kreuzberg. The city has three national operas, eight large orchestras, 880 choirs, approximately 260 art galleries and more than 200 theatres. In the 200 cinemas you will find Hollywood productions but also low budget art movies on offer. What more could you ask for?

Throughout history Berlin has always been known as a city open to the arts. Even during the times of Prussian Absolutism, Berlin was more liberal in spirit than any other of its neighbours. The 'Golden Twenties' are often singled out as the time when Berlin was the cultural capital of Europe. This is true but it does not give the whole picture if we only refer to this period. The arts are a mirror of the times, in which are also reflected in the many small theatres and art galleries. After Reunification there were new ideas but also discussions about funding for the arts. In this way the arts and politics cannot be easily separated.

Art treasures from many different centuries can be found in the many museums on the internationally famous Museumsinsel in the east of the city.

49. A bear's watchful eye on Ku'damm boulevard
50. A young couple at the Red Townhall

51. An important store on Friedrichstrasse road
52. The 206 quarter, with its Friedrichstadt walkways, shelters many offices and shops and is a witness to the architectural style of "Pei, Cobb, Freed and Partners".

Karl Friedrich Schinkel was commissioned by Friedrich Wilhelm III to build the Alte Museum (Old Museum) in 1823–1829. He wanted to show the whole world what treasures the royal palaces contained. This complex with an ornamental garden exhibits Old Master drawings, engravings and art from the GDR since 1945. 1855 saw the completion of the Neue Museum (New Museum) and then in 1876 the National Gallery was opened. Today it contains classical sculpture and paintings from the eighteenth to the twentieth century. In 1904 the Kaiser Friedrich Museum was built, renamed in 1958 the Bode Museum after its first director. The Pergamon Museum, containing the famous Zeus Altar from Pergamon in Turkey, opened in 1930. Next to it there is a collection of Islamic and East Asian antiquities. The Museumsinsel, with its magnificent collections, has recently been declared a World Heritage site by UNESCO and vast sums of money are being spent on its restoration and conservation.

53. The consumer's paradise in the 205 quartier was built according to the architect Oswald Mathias Ungers' drawings
54. A welcomed change: a coffee-break in the Scheunenviertel (the Barn quarter)
55. The "Berliner Zeitung" (The Berliner newspaper)

In fact the city has four big museum complexes of international status. After the Museumsinsel, Schloss Charlottenburg is certainly worth a visit as it has a great variety of treasures. Here you will find the Egyptian Museum with its well-known bust of Queen Nefertiti, as well as the Berggruen Collection with works by Picasso and Klee. The Schinkel Pavilion contains nineteenth century art. A third centre is in Dahlem, between Arnimallee and Landsstrasse, where the enormous Ethnological Museum is located. It has a special exhibition for blind visitors; and there is also the Museum of European Cultures nearby. The fourth complex is on the edge of the Tiergarten. It consists of an art gallery with paintings from the thirteenth to the eighteenth century, as well as a museum for musical instruments, and the famous Bauhaus Archive Museum of Design.

The Museum Haus at Checkpoint Charlie deals with Berlin's history as a divided city. It has an exhibition about the Wall, which tells the story of some spectacular

56. A sumptuous building on Friedrichstrasse: the Lafayette store

escapes, and there is also an old guardhouse and remnants of the Wall. The subject of National Socialism and GDR Socialism are dealt with at the Memorial to the German Resistance, the Anti-War Museum, the exhibition entitled 'Topography of Terror' in Stresemannstrasse, and in the Museum of Prohibited Art. There are many more museums and exhibitions to be seen in Berlin covering a great variety of subjects from sport, film history, and natural history to the more unconventional such as the Gay Museum or the Beate-Uhse Erotic Museum.

Famous for its architecture as well as its content is the Jewish Museum, designed by Daniel Libeskind, an American Jew. The form, the style and the interior design all represent one part of a philosophically influenced concept. The complex pays tribute to the millions of Jewish victims of the Terror. Rough zigzag lines on the façades remind us of the Star of David. Inside you will find empty rooms which have been blocked off in a manner to remind us of ravines. These areas are inaccessible to the visitor. Many paths lead to the Holocaust Room that has no windows.

57. An artistic glass construction gives the Lafayette store an unusual elegance

Following pages:
58. An impressing construction in the shape of a funnel near the Lafayette store

59. A "trabi": the standard car in old Eastern-Germany
60. During the times of the German Eastern-Western separation, the East-German government was based in the Republican Palace and was a source of national pride
61. Sand-filled bags at Checkpoint Charlie were used by people to protect themselves from gunshots
62. "You are leaving the American sector"; memorial at Checkpoint Charlie

Following pages:
63. The statue of Schiller (conceived by Reinhold Begas) in the Gendarmenmarkt (the Policemen's Market), immortalized by the great German poet

Another corridor will take you to the garden named after E T A Hoffmann. Concrete columns are geometrically arranged in a rectangular plan on a sloping site representing the exile forced upon thousands of Jews. The Jewish Museum, which is right next to the Berlin Museum, also deals with Jewish history by displaying objects that form part of a Jew's every day life in Berlin.

As was said before, Berlin offers exhibitions of art, culture and history unequalled by any other city in Germany. The symbol of the city, the Brandenburg Gate, is also a cultural memorial to history and to art. This internationally famous building stood in the centre of the divided city for 40 years. It stands in the former East Berlin close to the Reichstag, which was formerly in West Berlin, and has seen many important historical events. Military parades and demonstrations have passed through the Gate; in May 1945 the Soviets raised their flag here, and on 17 June 1953 the SED government ordered the shooting of 25 workmen who had fought for a better life.

64. Nocturnal view of the philharmonic
65. The Brandenburg Gate can be seen everywhere: from the window of an art gallery to the walkways of Friedrichstadt (Friedrichstadt-Passagen)
66. This museum was built by Karl Friedrich Schinkel and is one of the most beautiful classical museums in the world

Following pages:
67. The old National Gallery was conceived by Friedrich August Stüler between 1866 and 1876 and holds a large collection of paintings, some of which are by Max Liebermann

This masterpiece of classical architecture was inspired by the Acropolis and designed by Carl Gotthard Langhans. Built from 1788 to 1791, the city gate is framed by two guardhouses and ornamented with scenes from Greek mythology. The Quadriga on the gate, a symbol of peace, is now world famous. It was created by Johann Gottfried Schadow. During the French occupation, Napoleon took the Gate from Berlin but it returned in triumph in 1814, and has been standing here as a symbol of victory ever since. It can also be regarded as an outdoor museum. The splendid boulevard, Unter den Linden starts here and runs east to connect with the Museumsinsel in the river Spree.

68. A statue on the Museumsinsel (the Island of Museums)
69. The Castle of Charlottenburg (Charlottenburg Schloss), built in 1695, attracts thousands of tourists and shelters many varied museums
70. The Museum of Judaism was built under the supervision of Daniel Libeskind: its form, style and interior design are the materialization of a philosophical concept
71. The zig-zags carved into the wall and the design of the Museum of Judaism form a broken Star of David

The Wall: The most famous structure in Berlin has almost completely disappeared

'Ich bin ein Berliner' ('I am a citizen of Berlin')

72. The remains of the Wall in the Bernauer Strasse are reminders
of the once seperated city

73. Remains of the Wall in the Friedrichstrasse

All free men, from wherever they might be, are citizens of the City of West Berlin. That is why, as a free man, I am proud to say that: 'Ich bin ein Berliner.'

This quote is legendary and will never be forgotten. On 26 June 1963 President John F Kennedy spoke these historic words in front of Schönenberg City Hall. "I am a Berliner". He said it in German, which still guarantees him the love of many Germans today. Decades later, one of his successors, Ronald Reagan, at a meeting with Mikhail Gorbatchev, made a request for the Wall to be pulled down and for the Brandenburg Gate, the most important landmark in the city, to be reopened.

Today, at the beginning of the new millennium, it is almost impossible to imagine that a wall divided Berlin for 28 years. A group of young girls at a bus stop seem to confirm this thesis. "Is there anything left at all of the Wall?" they ask. No, there is nothing left of it, apart from a few memorial pieces in the city, kept as a reminder, and as a warning. You will find them in Schützenstrasse and in Bernauer Strasse, or at Potsdamer Platz where the first breakthrough from the West to the East was made in 1989 by the so-called 'Mauerspechte' (wall-peckers).

Photographs of those events were shown all over world: people equipped with only a hammer and a chisel, happy and laughing. They kept knocking at the Wall until chunks of stone came away. It was unbelievable to imagine that this was now possible. Even a few months previously, nobody would have dreamt that the Iron Curtain could have holes in it.

The complete demolition of the Wall and the checkpoints is regarded as an act of internal and external freedom. However, critics have pointed out that the city still struggles with its memories. Nevertheless now only a line of paving stones mark the former course of the 7.5 km long wall in and around Berlin; 106 km of concrete wall and a total of 45,000 segments of 2.75 tons in weight have been removed, as well as 127.5 km of fences and 302 watchtowers.

On 30 November 1990 the last piece of the inner-city wall in Weddinger Provinzstrasse was officially removed. It was 32.4 km long (including checkpoints). Many parts of the Wall were auctioned off and distributed throughout the world.

"Are they marching in?"

Let us leap 29 years back in time. It is Sunday, 13 August, 1961. At 1.11 am the East Berlin radio station interrupts its night time programme 'Melodies in the Night in order to bring a special announcement.

74. These paintings were only found on the western side of the Wall

"The governments of the Warsaw Pact countries have approached the representatatives of the GDR Government with the suggestion to establish a new order at the West Berlin border in order to prevent disturbances against the Socialist countries by establishing a suitable guard around the area of West Berlin." This rather wooden explanation simply means that the border will be closed and that West Berlin will be blocked off. But who listens to SED Radio anyway?

A few minutes after this broadcast the lights were extinguished at the Brandenburg Gate. Soldiers and tanks took their positions. Under the headlights of military vehicles, they began to rip up the roads and erect barbedwire blockades. The West still had no idea of the drama-tic changes that were about to take place in the border sectors. Only after messages had been received, the hams stopped running to the West and the military personnel were positionned at the border, was the police in west Berlin finally informed. 13,000 policemen were roused from their slumbers. A former senior policeman remembers the events at the Brandenburg Gate'.

At first we thought we would be invaded in West Berlin. However, they stopped exactly at the border sector". It was a precise military operation, which was led by a then quite unknown SED official, Erich Honecker. All the orders can be traced back to this 49-year-old. In those dramatic hours, a 10,500-strong task force consisting of policemen, the border police and members of combat teams were involved in making Berlin's separation complete. In addition there were several hundred members of the Stasi, the state security forces, and two motorised divisions of the National People's Army (NVA).

All together they amount- ed to 8,000 men, who received orders to approach the border, but keep 1 km away. Everything went according to plan. Only 12 out of 81 roads were left open. The rest were blocked with barbed wire. The trains and the underground services were interrupted. By August 23, only seven checkpoints were left: Friedrichstrasse, Bornholmer Strasse, Chausseestrasse, Invalidenstrasse, Heinrich-Heine-Strasse, Oberbaumbrücke,Sonnenallee and Friedrichstrasse-Zimmerstrasse (Checkpoint Charlie). The SED leader Walter Ulbricht had achieved his goal. The escape route to the West, through which more than 1.6 million GDR citizens had passed, had been closed.

75. Border-crossing at Checkpoint Charlie: Russian and American tanks arrived at this control point in 1961

76. Once a reality, today only but a memory: the fraternal kiss

President Kennedy goes sailing

The Mayor of West Berlin, Willy Brandt, was not in the city that night but on his way to an election rally: Brandt was the SPD candidate for Chancellor. As soon as he heard of the events, he flew back and drove to Potsdamer Platz and to the Brandenburg Gate.

Everywhere he saw the same scenes: builders, barricades, barbed wire, concrete columns and the GDR military. The same morning Brandt visited the Western City Commander in the leafy suburb of Dahlem. He wanted to know what the Western Allies intended to do about the situation. He met with a concerned silence. The Mayor was furious. He demanded that at the very least a protest should be made to Moscow and that there should be patrols along the border in order to reassure the people of West Berlin. All three City Commanders set out to execute this order. Otherwise, they did very little. They were waiting for instructions from their respective governments.

The US President, John F Kennedy, learned the news on board his yacht at 12.30 pm local time. At first he was furious that he had been informed at such a late stage. But he quickly calmed down and set off together with his Minister of Foreign Affairs, Dean Rusk, to organise a press conference. Afterwards he said: "Now I am going sailing. And you can go to your planned baseball game." The press release said: "The shutting off of East Berlin is a sign for the whole world to see that the Communist regime is failing. Before the whole world, the East German Ulbricht System is responsible for the inhuman isolation of their own people."

However Kennedy later confessed his relief to his friends. The Soviet President Khruschev would not have built a wall if "he really wanted the whole of Berlin". "This is not a good solution but a wall is a better idea than a war." Anyway, the three important corner stones of the American Berlin Policy had not been touched, namely one: the presence of Western Allies in Berlin, two: free access, and three: the right of self-determination for the citizens of West Berlin. Consequently there did not seem to be a need for any action by Washington.

"The West does nothing"

Soon the citizens of West Berlin begun to feel left in the lurch. On August 16 the *Bild Zeitung*, the largest tabloid newspaper, displayed this headline:

"The West does nothing". Mayor Willy Brandt challenged President Kennedy to act, otherwise trust in the Western Allies would be significantly shaken. In front of Schönenberg City Hall a demonstration of 300,000 people took place. The mood was heated. They lifted up banners with these words:"We need protection. Where are our protectors?" or "Betrayed by the West".

As President Kennedy continued to hear alarming reports, he answered with symbolic acts. He sent about 1,500 soldiers across the motorway from Helmstedt to Berlin in order to reinforce the US garrison. They were greeted with an exuberant welcome by the masses. Next, he sent his Deputy, Lyndon B Johnson, to the beleaguered city. Upon arrival at Tempelhof airport on August 19, he received an overwhelming welcome from the crowds. Hundreds of thousands lined-off the streets as he drove through the Western Sector.

In East Berlin a totally different image was presented. The GDR media broadcast extensive reports celebrated the event. The *New Germany Newspaper* wrote on August 14: "We can breathe out. Woe to those who misbehave". This is how workers from the capital and the GDR were quoted. In truth, there were also other voices.

Today we have access to previously secret SED reports. Here we read what the people really thought of the 'Protective Anti-fascist Wall'. On the morning of the August 13, an informant reports a woman who went screaming down the street urging everyone to come into the centre of the street in order to force a breakthrough. "We are Germans; we want to get to our German brothers." Others shout: "It is a disgrace that you commit yourselves to guard the border without letting us pass. You are not Germans." Without taking any notice of the general mood, the SED continued on their chosen path. They delt ruthlessly with the protestors and the first arrests were made.

The first casualties of the Wall

Countless GDR citizens were in a state of panic after the border was sealed off. They were trying to escape. What now followed was a macabre race between the refugees and the border police, who kept piling on the barbed wire. In spite of this 600 people, and that includes many families, managed to escape by the middle of September. The escapes via Bernauer Strasse were especially spectacular.

Several houses front the border sector. Many people from East Berlin were trying to escape through the flats here. They jumped out of the windows, or they tried to abseil. Some fell to their deaths and became the first casualties of the Wall.

On 24 September the police ordered 2,000 inhabitants to leave their homes in the Bernauer Strasse. In spite of this, many people from the East did not loose courage and attempted an escape. It was a tremendous risk, which sometimes cost them their lives. 230 people are documented as having died on the Berlin Wall, while more than 900 people died and 850 were injured attempting to cross the Wall or the inner German border.

Thousands failed and were imprisoned. Decades later they still suffer the consequences. German courts of law are still asking the question: Who is responsible? Those who gave the orders to shoot, or the marksmen? Or both of them? And to what extent? Up until the middle of 1999, there were 70 court cases. The history of the Wall is still being written.

Quiet Diplomacy

It is also thanks to quiet diplomacy that the border through Berlin and Germany now belongs to the past. Shortly after the building of the Wall, the first improvements were made. The SPD politician, Egon Bahr, is known for his slogan "change through outreach".

In December 1963 the first of many access pass agreements were made. 28 months later, the West Berlin people had access to visit their relatives in the Eastern half. In 1971 the telephone lines between both parts of the city were reconnected. In the same year, the four Allies signed the Berlin Quadripartite Agreement. This was a milestone for postwar Berlin. The important points were: recognition of the status quo in Berlin, the rejection of violence, and the Soviet promise to restore, or at least not to hinder, improvements in East-West road, rail, water and air traffic connections.

The Western Allies also recognized the status quo in East Berlin. The Berlin Agreement was signed a year later. It permitted people from the West to travel to East Berlin and the GDR. As a result communications between the Federal Republic and West Berlin become much easier.

By 1974 the Federal Republic had a permanent representative in East Berlin, the capital of the GDR. However, in the eighties there was growing dissatisfaction about the economic and political situation. Because of *glasnost* (Russian openness) and *perestroika* (the restructuring of the political and economic system), this dissatisfaction could no longer be suppressed.

Even the great festivities on 7 October 1989 to celebrate the 40th anniversary of the GDR could not distract attention from this reality. The Soviet President, Mikhail Gorbatchev, took part in the celebrations. He was obviously aware of this mood when he said: "Those who come too late, will be punished by life".

On 18 October the Politburo dismissed the Head of State and the Party, Erich Honecker. His successor was Egon Krenz. On 4 November million people, unimpressed by this change, demonstrated for democratic reform. On November 7 the entire GDR Government resigned from office. Hans Modrow became the new Minister President one day later.

Free Traffic

On the eve of 9 November Günter Schabowski, a Politburo member, prematurely announced the new government's decision to open the border. He had no idea of the consequences.

Suddenly tens of thousands East Berliners began to pour into West Berlin. During the following weekend, over one million people streamed into the West. When, after 28 years, the Brandenburg Gate was opened on 22 December , the symbolic separation had also come to an end. The former Chancellor, Helmut Kohl and the GDR Minister President, Hans Modrow, celebrated the opening at Paris Platz.

From Christmas Eve there was free traffic between both German States – without visas or the former obligatory currency exchange. US President, John F Kennedy sadly was not around any more. He would have liked it. His world famous words however remain: "Ich bin ein Berliner".

77. The "hall-of-death" located between the two walls
78. Crosses in memory of the victims of the wall

One third of Berlin consists of forest, water and recreational areas

'Pack your swimming trunks…'

79. Taking a rest on the Museumsinsel (the Island of Museums)
80. View from the Castle Bridge: a touristic boat on the Spree

Following pages:
81. On the boat, the wanderer passes by many touristic sites along the Spree

82. The House of International Cultures; the Berliners call it "Schwangere Auster" (pregnant oister)

Berlin is full of contrasts. On one side, there is busy traffic, skyscrapers and bustling crowds, on the other, there are oases of tranquillity, places for relaxation. It is unbelievable, but one third of Berlin is green. One example is the Tiergarten. This is not only a sector of Berlin, but it is the name for the largest park in the metropolis, situated in the centre of the city. The area covers 200 hectares of parkland, landscaped in the 1830s by Peter Joseph Lenné. After the Second World War, the Tiergarten was full of craters. Thanks to an intensive reforestation program, Berliners now again have an idyllic landscape.

Many statues commemorate remarkable artists and poets such as Goethe or Wagner. So the Tiergarten combines nature and recreation with art and culture. On the shores of the lake, Neuen See, and the canal, Landwehrkanal, you will find memorials to the murdered Spartakist leaders, Rosa Luxemburg and Karl Liebknecht. The exhibition of old gas lanterns near S-Bahnhof Tiergarten is also worth seeing.

This 'green lung' of the city was once a royal hunting ground. Next to the Breiten Allee (used for great parades during the Third Reich) is the Soviet Memorial. It was made of marble from the destroyed Neue Reichskanzlei.

In the middle of Strasse des 17 Juni you will find the bronze, 'Der Rufer' by Gerhard Marcks, but it is the Victory Column that dominates the area. On the base of this 70 m high column there is the bronze relief with scenes from some of Prussia's victorious wars, while there is a viewing platform 48 m up the column.

In the North of the Tiergarten there is an unusually designed congress hall, The House of Culture, known locally as 'The Pregnant Oyster'. In front of the building, reflected in a pool of water is the bronze sculpture by Henry Moore, 'Two Worlds'. Purchased at a cost of 1.8 million euros, this is currently the most expensive statue of the city.

The Cultural Forum, together with the Philharmonic Hall and the Gallery of European Art are to the south. Schloss Bellevue is on Am Spreeweg, which branches off the square, Grosser Stern, next to the Victory Column. The palace was built in 1785, and since 1994 it has been the residence of the Chancellor.

Of course there is also another attraction in Tiergarten. In the southwest part, the zoo with the world's largest selection of species is a magnet for visitors from all over the world. It first opened in 1844 and boasts over 15,000 animals.

Recreation in Grunewald

One of the most popular recreation grounds in Berlin is Wannsee, an delightful lake situated at the edge of Grunewald, and one of the largest inland waters in Europe.

This is a place for water sports, swimming, or just pure relaxation on the shore. There are quays with yachts. The swimming pool is further north. The lake has been open to the public since the early 1900s and has been continually improved and developed.

In the summertime thousands of people enjoy the sun here and there are luxurious cruise ships sailing the lake. A trip to the island, Schwanenwerder Insel with its opulent mansions makes a pleasant excursion.

One of the mansions, Inselstrasse 24–26, was built for the editor, Axel Springer. The Grunewald was previously a royal forest. Today it is crossed by the city motorway, Avus. A local landmark is the 55m high tower, the Grunewaldturm, by Franz Schwechten, built in neo-gothic style in 1897–98. The Teufelsberg is a 115m high hill, an artificial creation built of rubble. It boasts a radar station and the hunting lodge, Grunewald (1542), which is today a museum containing paintings and hunting weapons.

Only a few stops on the underground and you are amongst nature and away from all the crowds. It is always a good idea to make a little excursion, so long as the weather is agreable. Then it is like the old German folksong: "Pack your swimming trunks, take your little sister and run, all the way to Wannsee…"

83. The Bellevue Castle (Schloss Bellevue)

The New German Metropolis

The Centre of Power

84. The Reichstag (the parliament) is where the Bundestag (the federal government) is located

85. The symbol of the new Berlin: the dome of the Reichstag was built according to Britain's Norman Foster's infamous architectural project

"Take heed to the warning that the Republic has to be earned anew every day. Political culture and freedom does not happen by itself".

Helmut Kohl, Chancellor from 1982–1998

Where is the centre of power? The population can look down on the Parliament from a height of 50m made possible by the design of that most significant of historic buildings, the Reichstag. A lift will take you to the glass dome, which was designed by the famous British architect, Sir Norman Foster. There are 360 mirrors that reflect the light of the plenary assembly hall. From up here, one has an outstanding view over the city. Foster has managed to create a very modern parliament within the old external walls. Only in a few selected places do you have a glimpse of the original building. One of those remnants still visible is the graffiti left by Soviet soldiers. Otherwise modern art dominates the scene; for example 'The German Colours' by Gerhard Richter in the entry hall, and a floor relief by Ulrich Rückriem in the southern Lichthof, or Court of Light. On the south-entrance staircase paintings by Georg Baselitz are displayed, while the meditation room exhibits 'The Ten Commandments' by Günther Uecker.

86. The spiral stairs within the Reichstag's dome are climbed by hundreds of visitors every day. At the top, you get a panoramic view of the city
87. The central power: the Bundeskanzleramt (the residence of the Chancellor) in the Regierungsviertel (the governmental quarter)

The original copy of the German Law of May 23, 1949, is displayed in a glass cabinet in the visitors area.

But the greatest architectural achievement is the 23.5m high and 40m wide dome, which lights up in the darkness. The architect, Norman Foster, made 20 different preparatory designs for this roof. He wanted at all costs to avoid copying the old, destroyed historic fabric. The former dome was much larger. There was a great deal of political discussion regarding the roof. Eventually, a compromise was found. Now the dome has not only become a Berlin landmark, but one of the most popular tourist attractions. The visitor can walk up a spiral ramp all the way around the dome to the viewing platform.

On 19 April 1999 the German Bundestag opened the newly renovated Reichstag with a ceremonial meeting. The President of the Bundestag, Wolfgang Thierse, declared in his speech: 'As from now, Berlin is the political Metropolis of Germany (...)

In order to justify the purpose, for which the inner and outer structures of the Reichstag was built (...), we would like to thank the architect, Sir Norman Foster, who designed the rebuilding. He succeeded in creating a synthesis between the plenary assembly hall and the dome within the original historical structure. By means of creative building work, the syntheses reflects the house's history with its present and future. He was able to make the history visible, without remaining in it'. After this opening meeting, 125,000 visitors had the opportunity to inspect the Reichstag during a five day long opening celebrations. Huge crowds of people continue to pour into this historically significant building every day.

'In altogether bad taste'

In 1871, after the proclamation of the German Empire in the Hall of Mirrors in Versailles, the Prussian capital became also the new German capital.

The Parliament was now in need of a building for the representatives. In 1884 the Frankfurt architect, Paul Wallot, began building a gigantic neo-renaissance palace, whose glory reflected the Wilhelmine consciousness of power.

The building was finished in 1894; the pediment inscription 'For the German People' was ordered by Emperor Wilhelm II in 1916, in spite of the fact that he had earlier described the building as "in altogether bad taste". On 9 November 1918 the social democrat, Philipp Scheidemann declared the Republic whilst leaning out of a Reichstag's corner window. A year later, the Weimar Constitution came into force. From then on, the delegates were able to operate under democratic conditions.

On 27 February 1933 the Reichstag suffered great damage due to arson. Neither historians nor detectives have ever been able to discover who was really responsible for the fire. The National Socialists blamed the Communists in order to have an excuse to start a witch-hunt. Photographs taken in 1945 demonstrate the strong symbolic power that the Reichstag continued to have for the entire world;

they show a Soviet Flag as a symbol of German capitulation blowing on top of the building. The rebuilding programme of 1957–1972 did not include all the original decoration on the façade, nor did it restore the dome as in the original Wallot design. The GDR government was furious when the Reichstag was used as a background for especially selected Bundestag meetings, or sometimes for concerts. It was a worldwide media spectacle when the artists, Christo and Jeanne-Claude, wrapped the whole of the building in shining silver fabric.

Pompous Architecture

From the Reichstag's dome the visitor can look across to a new building which, even now after its completion, is still the object of great controversy in Germany: it is the Chancellor's Office. Critics say that it is out of proportion; it is too big, too pompous and inappropriate. Helmut Kohl, Chancellor until 1998, initiated the building work. His successor, who was not one of the supporters of this project, nevertheless took up office there.

The futuristically constructed building dominates the landscape of the Government Quartier. Axel Schultes and Charlotte Frank, the first prize winners in a 1992 architectural competition, designed the Chancellor's Office. The building work began in 1997. The Paul-Löbe-House, where the members of the Bundestag have their offices, is a stone's throw from there and also close to the Reichstag. The name of the building reminds us of the former Alsen Quartier, which developed around the Reichstag from 1840 onwards, and which was demolished by the National Socialists in 1938.

The Paul-Löbe-House, which also accommodates civil servants, is situated at the Spree Arch. Stephan Braunfels, who won the first prize in the realization competition in 1994, also won the architectural contract. The House offers 1,200 rooms for delegates, committees and archives. This 200m long building has been constructed in an open and transparent fashion.

Next door, in the Luisenblock, the Central Parliamentary Library and the Ministry of Science are located. All these buildings are favouring democracy at the beginning of the third millennium. One kilometre away, the remnants of Hitler's Reichskanzlei lie dormant beneath the surface.

A disputed move

The different ministry offices are housed in a variety of old and new buildings. Some of those addresses are no longer popular choices; for example the Ministry of Defence is in 'Bendlerblock', which was once home to the Commander-in-Chief of the armed forces. Col von Stauffenberg and some of his fellow conspirators in the plot against Hitler were shot in

The Ministry of Finance is located in Göring's former Ministry of Aviation. To relocate the government from Bonn, the former capital, to Berlin cost an estimated 20 billion DMs, which caused a lot of dispute among the political parties. The dispute was not entirely due to the great cost, but also to the fact that many ministers were afraid to move to Berlin.

One argument was that Bonn would suffer economically because of the move. Another argument was a historical one. The city could not boast a great democratic tradition, if you do not count the Weimar Republic. This is true when one remembers that the Nazi Terror was directly led from Wilhelmstrasse. It is said that Kaiser Wilhelm II called the Reichstag a 'monkey house'.

Then there is the delicate matter of East Berlin having been the capital of the GDR. On the other hand, the city on the Spree was the centre of resistance against Hitler and his government. The peaceful GDR revolution was also rooted in Berlin. Lastly, the present capital, with the help of the Western Allies, "has been writing the word democracy with capital letters" which means that Berliners have been making every effort to achieve it. However, when considered within a historical context, you are talking of a tender plant. The quotation from former Chancellor Kohl is therefore very relevant.

88. The house of Paul Loebe where the federal deputies work
89. Detailed view of the Bundeskanzleramt (residence of the Chancellor), which is sometimes compared to a washing machine

Karl Friedrich Schinkel
The Master Builder for eternity

The weekly paper, *Die Zeit* called him the builder of an "eternal Berlin". The sculptor, Christian Friedrich Tieck, represents him as a man of character, and a visionary, holding in his hand a sketch which points to his profession. The statue bears the simple inscription: "Karl Friedrich Schinkel (1781–1841)" and stands in Friedrichwerdersche Kirche, which Schinkel designed himself. This church is now part of the National Gallery exhibition (The Schinkel Museum). The church, with its elegant proportions, was built between 1824 and 1830. Originally, it was meant to be Berlin's first neo-gothic building. It has only one main part, the nave, but two church towers, and so reminds us of the design of an English university church. In the Second World War the interior was largely destroyed. At present, this building serves as a sculpture gallery, showing works from the Renaissance to the nineteenth century, including works by Schadow, Schinkel and others. There are also paintings of Schinkel's builds that were destroyed during the Second World War.

Fortunately there are still many buildings by Schinkel that did survive more or less as built. There is the Alte Museum am Lustgarten which was opened in 1830. It has a long row of columns, which makes it the ideal introduction to the renowned Museumsinsel. A few yards from there is the Schlossbrücke, the bridge built in 1824, and the Neue Wache, or New Watch House, situated on the Unter den Linden and built six years previously. In 1989, what had formerly been a place for the guards of honour of the National People's Army became the Federal Republic's central memorial. Even the Protestant cathedral, the Berliner Dom, with its 85m high copper-plated dome, carries Schinkel's signature.

A genuine multi talent

This master builder has gone down in history as a multi talent; he was an architect, a conservator of monuments and a city planner all at the same time; he designed remarkable stage scenery, for example for Mozart's *The Magic Flute*; painted romantic scenery, and also made his living as a furniture designer. However, his masterpiece has to be the Theatre at the Gendarmenmarkt, now the Concert Hall. It is literally framed by the Französischer Dom and the Deutsche Dom. The building is a feast for the eyes, especially at night when it is bathed in warm light, and is a masterpiece of classical architecture. Many think that this is the most beautiful area in Berlin. Friedrich Wilhelm III ordered the building of this theatre, which is now frequently used for concerts by the Berlin Philharmonic Orchestra. It was built between 1818–1821 on precisely the same place where the National Theatre had stood before; this building having burnt down in 1817. Schinkel also designed all the interiors, but reused the colonnade of the old theatre. The Theatre was damaged in the Second World War and, it was rebuilt as a concert hall. However, the façades are still true to the original design. As it used to be the custom, there are different entrances for the different social classes. Ionic columns flank the staircase leading to the entrance for the middle classes. The upper class had a separate entrance next to the driveway for the state coaches. In front of this splendid building by Schinkel there is a white marble statue in honour of the famous poet Schiller. The work of Reinhold Begas, the statue was taken down by the National Socialists in the thirties but reinstated by the GDR government in 1988. The statue's plinth is ornamented with inscriptions from philosophy, history and theatre.

Yet, Karl Friedrich Schinkel built even more memorable works; the Humboldt Schloss in Tegel, and the Klein-Glienicke Schloss for example were all his creations. There is also the iron War Memorial surviving at Kreuzberg. The former Schinkel Building Academy, erected in front of the Friedrichwerdersche Kirche in 1836, was badly damaged in the War and in 1962 was demolished by the GDR State Department. Of course, since 1991 the State Department building has also vanished. Schinkel was buried in Dorotheenstädtische Friedhof along side many other prominent Berliners.

90. Fountain in front of the Altes Museum, which was built by the renowned architect Schinkel

91. The dome of the Reichstag (the parliament)